Meal on a Page

By

Tania Melkonian

Praise for the Meal on a Page Cookbook

"This game-changing resource stands apart from the sea of cookbooks because it is specifically designed to demystify the process of meal creation and set you up for success. As a practitioner who has witnessed the power of these recipes to resolve chronic illness, malaise, and medication dependence, this guide is at the top of my list for personal empowerment, and endorsed as a Vital Mind Reset approved guide!"

KELLY BROGAN, M.D.

NY Times Bestselling author and founder of Vital Mind Reset

"If what has stood as an obstacle between you and healthful meals is the business of cooking them, with the MEAL ON A PAGE cookbook Tania Melkonian has swept away such obstacles. I have always been comforted by Tania's food, not only because it is delicious and innovative but because it confirms that nature's prescriptions are laid out before us on our cutting boards. We need only a little guidance and a compelling invitation. With stunning photographs, clear almost info-graphical recipes and a built in timeline, MEAL ON A PAGE offers such an invitation."

SAYER JI, CEO and founder of Greenmedinfo author of bestseller, *Regenerate: Unlocking your Body's Radical Resilience through the New Biology*

"In my profession I am always considering time, space and function simultaneously and in relationship to one another. Yet, somehow I am not very good at juggling tasks in the kitchen - that includes making a multi-course meal efficiently! Thankfully, in the Meal on a Page Cookbook, Tania Melkonian has shared her superpower by creating this genius new method for cooking a complex meal with ease: It's kitchen choreography!"

GILAD SHOHAM, inventor and industrial designer and Founder of Medonyx inc.

"This book is simply brilliant. Beautiful, original recipes put together in an easy, unique format. Perfect for a novice cook to get guidance on how to navigate cooking an entire meal (or just one dish if she prefers!) or for the more experienced foodie. As a Chef, I appreciated the offer of scratch recipes for base ingredients and as a food lover I welcomed the visual reference of the spectacular photographs!"

GILLIAN BLASDALE-HOLMES, Chef at Wylde Green Kitchen, England

Introduction

Preparing food has become a chore, the domain of celebrities, too time-consuming, too labor-intensive or just boring. The new food landscape deifies chefs and makes food prepared by somebody else exotic and favorable. I don't suggest that we should not enjoy meals in restaurants or even a take-out experience once in a while. I am even in favor of the occasional prepared food item supplementing a home-cooked meal. It is when these occasions become chronic in our lives that the perilous chasm widens. I refer to the chasm separating simply eating food and experiencing a meal.

In the short term, separating our palates from our preparation of food seems more convenient and more interesting. In the long term however, it proves to be far less so - certainly financially. A typical chain restaurant in the US will offer a main course of salmon, side of vegetables and rice and dessert for an average of $25.00 USD (not including gratuity and other charges). Even if we were to consider price as the only advantage, a home cooked meal still wins by a substantial margin: an equivalent home-cooked meal totals about $10-$12. Of course, the financial is not the only advantage and may not even be the most important one.

There is plenty written about the nutritional superiority of food we source ourselves and dishes whose contents and assembly we can deftly control. And yet WE STILL DON'T COOK! So even if you feel exhausted by the regular barrage of experts opining on this moment's superfood or which adaptogen to replace your coffee with, the potential for store bought or restaurant prepared food to contain damaging amounts of sugar, salt and additives cannot be denied.

Also, I know it takes some effort to prepare food. It is possible that what we gain in nutrition and fiscal profit we bear in the cost of our time. But, in making that commitment, we secure an unexpected payoff. The return on our investment is not only a more affordable meal free of unwanted preservatives and other additives, but one whose flavors are robust and complex; The biggest return on the time investment is in the unveiling of the magic of transforming food into a meal - an experience. And what if - once you make a reasonable commitment of time and accept that some effort will have to be learned or re-learned - that the guidance to make this unveiling easy is just a turn of a page away?

Preparing meals rather than just individual recipes allows the stories of food to be explored. Putting dishes together inspires appetizing menus, ignites conversations, begins cultural explorations and propels health missions. On the pages of this book, you will find EIGHT stories as a starting point to tell countless more.

The MEAL ON A PAGE format is unique in that it provides a time management reference that has already been calculated. It's really a recipe for an entire meal - not just one dish. It's a how-to for wholistic dining in the literal sense. Please use this book to reclaim your meals and be the master of transforming your ingredients into experiences.

~Tania

How to use this book

A few cooking fundamentals apply. Below find a couple of lists with suggestions ....and, well, stronger suggestions on what to have as part of your kitchen tool inventory

Need to have

- Chef's knife - this is your most versatile knife. Invest In a good one and keep it sharp. Cooking is miserable with a dull or bad knife (not to mention dangerous!) Chef's knives come in lengths 6-14 inches. Choose one whose blade is roughly the length of your forearm (elbow to wrist).

- Paring knife - small knife for detailed work.

- Serrated knife - to help get through thicker casings to softer insides (like tomatoes, bread and bell peppers)same length of your chef knife.

- Food processor & attachments.

- Metal colander.

- At least 1 medium (24 cm/9 inches) skillet (frying pan) or sauté pan with lid (a frying pan has sloped sides while a sauté pan has straight sides). Either will work for the recipes in this book and will be referred to interchangeably as well.

- At least 1 pot with lid large enough to contain 8 cups/2 liters. That is what is meant by 'large pot' for the purposes of the recipes in this book.

- At least 2 medium sized pots with lids.

- Vegetable peeler.

- Pastry brush- or dedicated small soft bristle paint-brush for the kitchen.

- Springform or other easy-release cake pan.

- At least 1 large baking sheet.

- Parchment (greaseproof) paper.

- Measuring cups.

- Measuring spoons.

- A couple of large mixing bowls.

- Wooden spoon.

- Large spatula.

- Whisk.

- Blender.

- The largest cutting board you can fit on your kitchen - plastic ones are the most sanitary but tend to warp. Wooden ones are the kindest to your knife blade sharpness and give you the most control. From a food sanitation point of view, however, they are less efficient than plastic. Glass cutting boards are the worst - don't go there!

Nice to have

- Immersion blender - stick-shaped.

- Vegetable spiralizer.

- Mandolin.

- Stand mixer - fancy.

- Hand mixer- less fancy but a whisk will do in place of either of these (more muscle work though!).

- Spice grinder or mortar pestle - Having one of these will give you the facility to use whole spices and grind them yourself.

Before starting on a recipe, prepare your ingredients. Assume room temperature unless otherwise indicated. Ingredients should be measured and prepared as per the way they are listed in the ingredient list. For example, if the recipe calls for "½ cup walnuts, chopped" you would measure half a cup of walnuts and then chop them. Conversely, if the ingredient is listed "½ cup of chopped walnuts" then you would fill a half-cup measuring device with ½ cup of already chopped nuts. Lay out all the ingredients and have them ready before you start. The culinary (read French) term for this is mise en place which means 'put in place'.

Big player ingredients

Oils

The following oils are recommended and all have their benefits dependent on the recipe. Olive oil is the one I use the most frequently but imparts a taste which some don't care for. Coconut oil has a distinct taste as well but is very stable at high temperatures. Avocado oil is a good option if you want a tasteless oil but it's only so when refined. Red palm oil is also very stable and has a mild taste but imparts a strong orange color. Most recipes in this book you can use your preferred oil. It is indicated in the recipe when a particular oil is required or preferred.

Onions

Onions are aromatics and are at the heart of virtually every savory recipe's flavor base. Onions make you cry when they are raw. There are many varieties but generally speaking - red onions, yellow and Vidalia are less pungent than white ones. Shallots are small, sweet mild onions.

Salt

Salt is absolutely essential for the prepared cook. Buy good quality pink rock salt (Himalayan or Hawaiian) or sea salt. Skip iodized versions. Sea salt already has iodine and rock salt is a mineral itself.

Black garlic

Black garlic is garlic that has been essentially cooked super slowly and at very low heat. It has more anti-oxidant power than fresh garlic and tastes completely different. Black garlic is sweet, chewy and less assaulting to the palate. If you are not a garlic lover, try black garlic. If your cooking has been based on the principle that one cannot have enough garlic, then meet your new favorite ingredient. Either way, you win! It's worth sourcing black garlic paste but you can also buy black garlic bulbs and squish them out of the clove casing when you need them. Black garlic tastes like a sweet, thick balsamic vinegar with more depth.

Spices

Spices Buying organic spices will ensure they have not been blasted with radiation, a practice that is purported to keep spices and some other foods subjected to this process clean. In the US the regulating food safety body (USDA) does not allow irradiation on organic foods. Recipes in this book call for specific spices but you will learn your preferences and, truly, there is no wrong way to use a spice if you find you like it. Ones that I can't live without are: cumin, turmeric, allspice and cinnamon. Herbs that I use dry: oregano, thyme and sage.

◼ Pomegranate

Pomegranate Many recipes in this book call for pomegranate in one of Its many delicious, nutritionally potent, beautiful iterations. I have an online tutorial on how to open up a pomegranate and take out the arils (the name for the pomegranate's fruit seeds) but it's also easily available already broken down.

A word about heat

Oven temperatures are indicated in Fahrenheit. 350F = 177C. 400F = 200C

On an electrical stove, markings are often indicated as SIMMER/LOW (or MIN), MEDIUM, HIGH

Gas mark equivalents are SIMMER/LOW =1-2; MEDIUM = 3-5, MEDIUM/HIGH = 6-7, HIGH = 8+

The colours correspond to recipes.

For example, all the ingredients in the green box and all the instructions in green column correspond to the recipe for ON THE CUTTING VEG PARFAIT.

All the ingredients in the yellow box correspond to the recipe for LENTIL SWEET POTATO GREEN CUPS and all the ingredients in the **maroon** box correspond to the IMAM BAYALDI-STUFFED EGGPLANT.

Minute markers indicate how much time should have elapsed to keep the cook on track.

60 min

All recipes in Meal On A Page yield 2 servings. For 4 servings, double the quantities.

For example, for 4 servings of Lentil Sweet Potato Cups, use 2 tablespoons of olive oil, 2 teaspoons of oregano and 2 avocados.. etc.

Cooks read down the column following the instructions as with a traditional recipe in numerical order. The MEAL ON A PAGE format calculates the timing and orders the instructions in such a way that THREE dishes in the meal are ready once the cook reaches the end of the page.

In the example, instruction 1 corresponds to IMAM BAYALDI-STUFFED EGGPLANT, instruction 2 corresponds to LENTIL SWEET POTATO GREEN CUPS recipe, and instruction 3 corresponds to ON THE CUTTING VEG PARFAIT recipe.

Ingredients In ***bold italic underline*** indicate an additional recipe is offered on a separate page to give the option to make a scratch version.

The unique MEAL ON A PAGE format allows cooks to retain the option of preparing just one or two of the recipes in the meal by following only the directions of the corresponding colour(s).

For example, to prepare only the IMAM BAYALDI-STUFFED EGGPLANT dish, the cook would follow the instructions- corresponding to **maroon** colour only-in numerical order.

Imam bayildi - stuffed eggplant

- 1 large Italian eggplant
- *2 fire roasted or pickled red peppers*
- 4 tablespoons tomato paste
- 2 cloves garlic
- 1 teaspoon zataar seasoning (or 1 teaspoon dried thyme)
- Sea salt to taste
- 1 teaspoon olive oil

Lentil sweet potato green cups

- 1 large organic sweet potato - scrubbed very well
- 1 cup grated organic carrots
- 1 medium white onion, peeled
- 1 cup dried green or brown lentils
- 1 tablespoon olive oil
- 1 teaspoon dried oregano
- 1 avocado
- 8 large kale leaves of equal size, washed
- ½ teaspoon black garlic paste
- 1 teaspoons sea salt

On the cutting veg parfait

- 1 cup white cauliflower florets
- 1 cup grated organic carrots
- ½ cup sliced almonds
- 1 teaspoon ground cardamom
- ½ cup coconut or nut milk
- 1 cup dried cherries
- 1 cup chopped dried apricot
- 1 very ripe banana

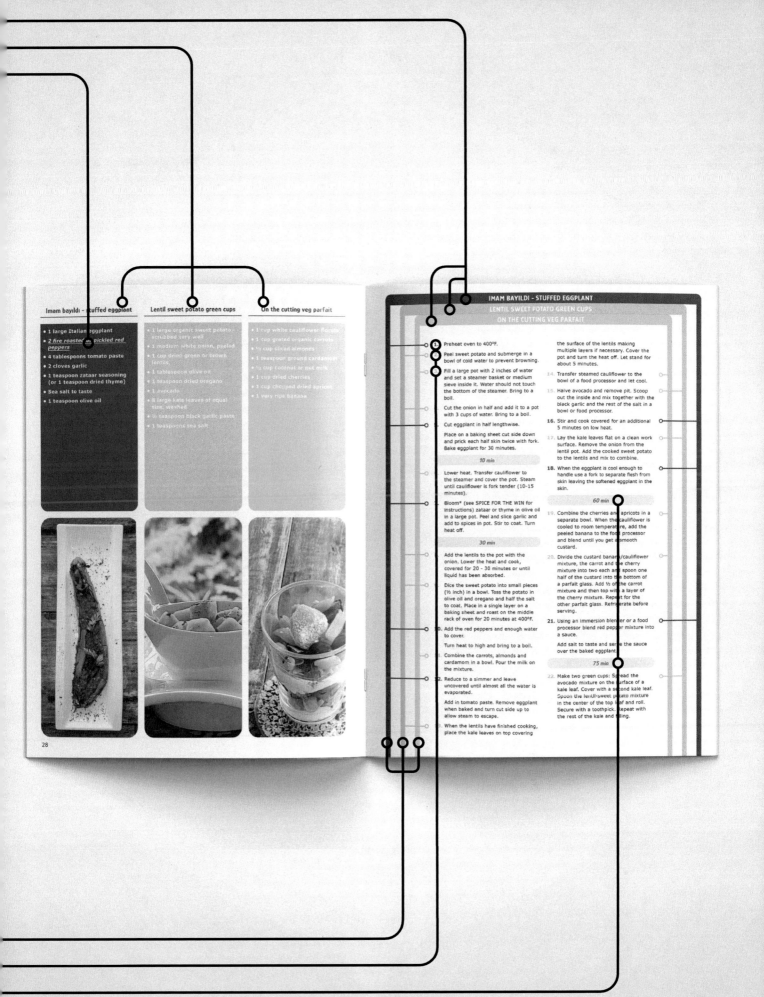

1. Preheat oven to 400°F.

2. Peel sweet potato and submerge in a bowl of cold water to prevent browning.

3. Fill a large pot with 2 inches of water and set a steamer basket or medium sieve inside it. Water should not touch the bottom of the steamer. Bring to a boil.

   Cut the onion in half and add it to a pot with 3 cups of water. Bring to a boil.

   Cut eggplant in half lengthwise.

   Place on a baking sheet cut side down and prick each half skin twice with fork. Bake eggplant for 30 minutes.

   10 min

   Lower heat. Transfer cauliflower to the steamer and cover the pot. Steam until cauliflower is fork tender (10-15 minutes).

   Bloom* (see SPICE FOR THE WIN for instructions) zataar or thyme in olive oil in a large pot. Peel and slice garlic and add to spices in pot. Stir to coat. Turn heat off.

   30 min

   Add the lentils to the pot with the onion. Lower the heat and cook, covered for 20 - 30 minutes or until liquid has been absorbed.

   Dice the sweet potato into small pieces (½ inch) in a bowl. Toss the potato in olive oil and oregano and half the salt to coat. Place in a single layer on a baking sheet and roast on the middle rack of oven for 20 minutes at 400°F.

10. Add the red peppers and enough water to cover.

    Turn heat to high and bring to a boil.

11. Combine the carrots, almonds and cardamom in a bowl. Pour the milk on the mixture.

12. Reduce to a simmer and leave uncovered until almost all the water is evaporated.

    Add in tomato paste. Remove eggplant when baked and turn cut side up to allow steam to escape.

13. When the lentils have finished cooking, place the kale leaves on top covering

the surface of the lentils making multiple layers if necessary. Cover the pot and turn the heat off. Let stand for about 5 minutes.

14. Transfer steamed cauliflower to the bowl of a food processor and let cool.

    Halve avocado and remove pit. Scoop out the inside and mix together with the black garlic and the rest of the salt in a bowl or food processor.

16. Stir and cook covered for an additional 5 minutes on low heat.

17. Lay the kale leaves flat on a clean work surface. Remove the onion from the lentil pot. Add the cooked sweet potato to the lentils and mix to combine.

18. When the eggplant is cool enough to handle use a fork to separate flesh from skin leaving the softened eggplant in the skin.

    60 min

19. Combine the cherries and apricots in a separate bowl. When the cauliflower is cooled to room temperature, add the peeled banana to the food processor and blend until you get a smooth custard.

20. Divide the custard banana/cauliflower mixture, the carrot and the cherry mixture into two each and spoon one half of the custard into the bottom of a parfait glass. Add ½ of the carrot mixture and then top with a layer of the cherry mixture. Repeat for the other parfait glass. Refrigerate before serving.

21. Using an immersion blender or a food processor blend red pepper mixture into a sauce.

    Add salt to taste and serve the sauce over the baked eggplant

    75 min

22. Make two green cups: Spread the avocado mixture on the surface of a kale leaf. Cover with a second kale leaf. Spoon the lentil-sweet potato mixture in the center of the top leaf and roll. Secure with a toothpick. Repeat with the rest of the kale and filling.

WARM WEATHER WINNER

TO PREPARE THIS MEAL

YOU WILL NEED

- ☐ **Walnuts**
- ☐ **Shallots**
- ☐ **Parsley**
- ☐ **Olive oil**
- ☐ **Lemon**
- ☐ **Salmon**
- ☐ **Spices**
- ☐ **Red peppers**
- ☐ **Tomatoes**
- ☐ **Cucumber**
- ☐ **Vegetable stock**

- ☐ **Garlic & balsamic vinegar OR black garlic**
- ☐ **Tangerine**
- ☐ **Stock**
- ☐ **Sherry vinegar**
- ☐ **Can coconut milk**
- ☐ **Pineapple**
- ☐ **Coconut or avocado oil**
- ☐ **Pineapple**
- ☐ **Matcha powder**

- ☐ **Food processor**
- ☐ **Blender**
- ☐ **Parchment paper**
- ☐ **Baking sheet**
- ☐ **2 skillets/pans**
- ☐ **Food processor**

Brain-pop pesto crusted fish

- ½ cup walnut pieces
- 1 large shallot
- 1 bunch organic Italian
- parsley, washed and dried
- ½ tablespoon olive oil
- 1 teaspoon sea salt
- Juice of ½ lemon
- 2 skinless filets of wild salmon, each about an inch thick at center

Gaspachoscuro

- 1 teaspoon each of:
- paprika, garlic granules, cumin, black pepper, thyme
- 1 teaspoon olive oil
- 4 whole pickled or fire-roasted red peppers
- 4 large roma tomatoes
- 1 medium cucumber, sliced lengthwise
- 3 cloves black garlic or ½ tablespoon black garlic paste (or 1 clove garlic and 1 teaspoon balsamic vinegar)
- 1 peeled tangerine
- 3 scallions or green onions
- 1 teaspoon sherry vinegar
- *1 cup vegetable stock*
- 1 cup coconut water (set aside from grilled pineapple recipe) or 1 additional cup vegetable stock

Grilled pineapple with coconut matcha cream

- 2 one inch thick fresh cored pineapple rings
- ½ teaspoon coconut oil
- 1 can full fat coconut milk (refrigerated overnight)
- 1 teaspoon unsweetened matcha (green tea powder)

1. In a small skillet bloom spices in olive oil. Remove from heat. *(See SPICE FOR THE WIN to learn to bloom spices).*

2. Preheat oven to 375°F.

3. Spoon out top thick layer of coconut cream from the can (photo on next page) and set aside coconut water remaining in the can for the gazpacho recipe or another use.

4. Add remaining gaspacho ingredients to a high speed blender and blend on highest setting until well combined.

5. In a food processor, pulse walnut pieces until a paste-like texture is attained. Scrape the sides and bottom of the bowl to loosen the paste.

6. Add bloomed spices to blender. Pulse a few times until incorporated and refrigerate until time to serve.

20 min

7. Peel and roughly chop the shallot and add to food processor. Process until combined.

8. Set medium sized skillet on low heat. Add coconut oil.

9. Add parsley, oil, ½ teaspoon of salt and lemon and mix until combined, stopping the food processor and scraping the sides and bottom of the bowl as necessary. If the mixture is too dry, add warm water slowly until it holds together but does not crumble.

10. Turn skillet with oil to medium high heat and add pineapple rings.

11. Pat salmon dry and sprinkle with remaining salt. Place on a parchment-lined baking sheet. Add half of walnut mixture to each of the filets of salmon, placing it in a ball on top of the center of the filet. With finger pads, work the paste to even thickness pushing to the edges of the salmon filet. Cover the top surface of each filet with an even layer of walnut paste.

40 min

12. Once the pineapple becomes aromatic, flip with a spatula. Grill second side of pineapple until aromatic.

13. Place the baking sheet on middle rack and bake, uncovered for 6 minutes for medium doneness (bake an additional 2 minutes for well done salmon). Turn the oven off.

60 min

14. Remove pineapples from heat.

15. Add matcha powder to the coconut cream and stir to combine.

16. After one minute turn oven broiler on to high and broil for an additional 2 minutes. Serve right away.

17. Add pineapple rings to a plate and a dollop of coconut matcha cream to the center of each ring. Serve right away.

Warm Weather Winner
Versatile vegetable stock

Making anything from scratch does require more time than it takes to open a packet. However, the active time - the time spent actually expending effort - for stock is relatively low. It's prep intensive (though much less intensive the way I do it!) And then patience takes over as the main ingredient while the simmering binds flavors together. Moreover, making-versus buying-stock gives you more control over the source and quality of the ingredients used. This is of importance for flavor and for nutritional advantage, especially when it comes to additions like salt which is heavily used in commercially processed stock. Another aspect of scratch-cooking which I find advantageous is that it provides a great way to mitigate waste. I use stock-making sessions (which I initiate about once every two weeks or so) as an opportunity to give peelings, seeds, skins and other under-dog ingredients a second chance to make a flavor difference!

Several recipes in this book call for vegetable stock including the gazpacho in WARM WEATHER WINNER so named for its cooling qualities. Using stock in place of water to cook rice, pasta and sauces adds depth to the flavor.

I've developed a few short-cuts which I am thrilled to be able to pass on to interested cooks which will cut the prep time down even more. My hope is that these hacks will - rather than encouraging indolence -inspire you to use the time saved for creative pursuits in the kitchen!

YOU WILL NEED:

- 4-6 cups water (enough to fill your largest pot about 2/3 full)
- 3 onions, trimmed, peeled and quartered
- 3 celery stalks, roughly chopped
- 3 carrots, trimmed and peeled or scrubbed well
- Any vegetable peelings leftover from the preparation of previous recipes (for example parsley or fennel stalks, fennel fronds, almond or beet skins, asparagus bases, eggplant peel....)
- Quick herb infusion shortcut!

QUICK HERB INFUSION - SHORTCUT!

In a bowl, combine the following WHOLE spices (ground spices are not suitable for this application)

1 teaspoon each of - black or pink peppercorn, cumin seeds, coriander or fenugreek seeds

Using back of a wooden spoon or mortar pestle roughly 'break' the spice pods or seeds

INSTRUCTIONS

1. Add all ingredients to a large pot and bring to a boil

2. Reduce heat, cover and allow to simmer for about 45 minutes.

3. Remove lid and skim off any bubbly matter that has accumulated on the surface

4. Simmer, uncovered for another 10 minutes

5. Strain the liquid from stock and store in the refrigerator for up to two weeks or in the freezer for up to 3 months.

FANCY FRENCH

TO PREPARE THIS MEAL YOU WILL NEED

- ☐ Ghee or oil
- ☐ Zucchini / courgette
- ☐ Caraway or fennel seeds
- ☐ Cashew (or other) cream cheese
- ☐ Dill
- ☐ Almond (or other) ricotta
- ☐ Spices
- ☐ Halibut
- ☐ Olives

- ☐ Green beans
- ☐ Carrots
- ☐ Caperberries / capers
- ☐ Olive oil
- ☐ Macadamia nuts
- ☐ Shredded coconut
- ☐ Cocoa
- ☐ Dates
- ☐ Raspberries
- ☐ Brewed Coffee
- ☐ Parchment paper

- ☐ 2 Ramekins or 6 inch springform
- ☐ Food processor
- ☐ Vegetable peeler
- ☐ 2 Baking sheets
- ☐ Mixing bowl

Zucchini stuffed with herbed ricotta

- 1 large zucchini
- ¼ teaspoon fennel or caraway seeds
- 1 bunch fresh dill, finely chopped
- 1 cup almond ricotta or similar (any 'fresh' nut or dairy cheese can be used here)

Fish Parcels

- 2 large carrots - scrubbed well or peeled
- 2 wild halibut steaks (4x5 inches wide/long,1 inch thick)
- 1 teaspoon sea salt
- ½ teaspoon black pepper
- 1 tablespoon ghee (see RETURN TO RIVIERA for how to make ghee) or olive oil
- 2 tablespoons brined caperberries
- ¼ cup pitted chopped black olives
- 1 cups trimmed green beans
- Juice of 1 lemon
- Two 8x11 inch squares of parchment paper

Chocolate raspberry dairy-free cheesecake

- ½ cup raw or toasted macadamia nuts
- ¼ cup unsweetened shredded coconut
- *1 cup unsweetened cashew cream cheese*
- ¼ cup pure cocoa powder
- 4 dates (more for a sweeter filling) soaked in water for 30 minutes, drained
- 2 tablespoons cooled brewed espresso coffee
- 1 cup fresh raspberries

1. Preheat oven to 350F.

2. Cut zucchini lengthwise, de-seed and discard seeds. Place cut side down on a baking sheet.

15 min

3. Using a vegetable peeler, create carrot curls (as shown in photos, next page).

4. Once oven comes to temperature, bake zucchini for 10 minutes.

5. Combine macadamia nuts and coconut in food processor and pulse until sand-like in texture.

6. Press ½ the mixture firmly into the bottom of each of two 3 inch diameter service vessels (can use an individual tart tin, ramekin, coffee cup etc). Wider the base means a thinner crust. Freeze for 20 minutes. Rinse food processor.

7. Put a small saucepan on medium heat. Add fennel/caraway seeds to the dry pan and toast until aromatic (about a minute) and remove from heat.

8. Combine all remaining ingredients except raspberries in a food processor and process until smooth. Remove crust from the freezer and top with 'cheese' mixture. Return to freezer for at least another 20 minutes.

9. In a bowl combine almond ricotta, dill and toasted seeds.

40 min

10. **Make fish parcels:** Place one piece of parchment horizontally on work surface. Place a halibut steak at the centre of parchment, also horizontally (skin side down if skin has not been removed) and season with salt and pepper. Drizzle each piece with ½ the oil or ghee. Arrange the rest of the ingredients on work surface in listed order like an assembly line, with carrot curls last.

    Place ½ of the quantity of each of the ingredients on top of each halibut steak. Drizzle with ½ the lemon juice. Bring the two long edges of the paper together at the top and center of contents. Fold over twice until the contents are tightly wrapped lengthwise. Take the two corners of each of the shorter edges and fold in to each other to seal the packet and

then fold down tightly underneath the fish (pictured on next page) Transfer to baking sheet. Repeat with the remaining fish and ingredients.

11. Turn zucchini cut side up on serving plate and fill with ricotta mixture. Serve.

12. Using a fork, punch two sets of holes in the top of each parchment packet. Place baking sheet on the middle rack of the oven. Bake for 15 - 20 minutes. Open packets carefully when serving as steam will escape!

60 min

13. Remove cheesecakes from freezer and let stand for about 5 minutes until surface softens a little. Arrange 1/2 cup raspberries on top of each cake pushing them into surface to hold them in place. Serve.

FANCY FRENCH: CASHEW CHEESE
The non-dairy answer to your cheese-tooth

Non-dairy cheeses are a great, high protein option for anyone choosing a plant-based or dairy free-diet but offer a unique flavor worth experiencing even if dairy is part of your diet. Two non-dairy cheeses feature in this meal on a page, FANCY FRENCH, showing the versatility of nut-based cheeses. In some cultures consuming dairy and fish or seafood together is not appropriate. So, bookending our fish parcels with the ZUCCHINI STUFFED WITH HERB RICOTTA and CHOCOLATE-RASPBERRY 'CHEESECAKE' seems like an efficient way to maintain cheese-loving French cuisine as an inspiration for this meal on a page without any lactose related violations!

Both of the 'cheeses' featured in this meal are alternatives to fresh, uncultured cheeses (vs. cultured, hard cheeses like Cheddar, Gouda or Provolone for example). We will focus on the cashew cream cheese that forms the filling of the CHOCOLATE RASPBERRY CHEESECAKE. Other nuts can be substituted for cashews; almonds, Macadamia or Brazil nuts work well. I have had the most success achieving a creamy texture with cashews, however.

Nuts should be raw and unsalted. Soak them for at least 2 hours or overnight. The longer the nuts soak, the tangier, more cheese-like the flavor will be. For a fresher taste soak for the minimum time so that nuts are soft enough to blend but not too sour.

Drain and rinse nuts before making your cheese. Discard the soaking water.

After soaking, use 2 cups fresh water for every ¾ cup of soaked nuts (volume of nuts will increase in size when soaked).

2 cups water: ¾ cup soaked nuts will yield about 1 cup of 'cream cheese' which is what you need for the CHOCOLATE-RASPBERRY CHEESECAKE.

There are only 2 ingredients in the cheese, but the process is particular. You will need a powerful blender. Pour ¼ the quantity of water in the blender first and start the blender on low speed. Add ¼ of the nuts and gradually increase speed of blender. Keep alternating the addition of water and nuts as you gradually increase speed to high until a creamy texture is achieved scraping down the sides of the blender occasionally. The gradual increase in speed is important to encourage the nuts and water to emulsify. If the desired consistency is reached before all the water is used, there is no need to use all of it.

*the above recipe yields a neutral tasting cream cheese. For a mildly sweet cheese add dates (as is called for in the CHOCOLATE-RASPBERRY CHEESECAKE recipe). For a savory cream cheese, add ½ teaspoon each of garlic powder and salt for every 1 cup of cream cheese you are making and substitute apple-cider vinegar for ½ the quantity of water.

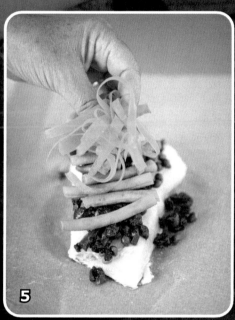

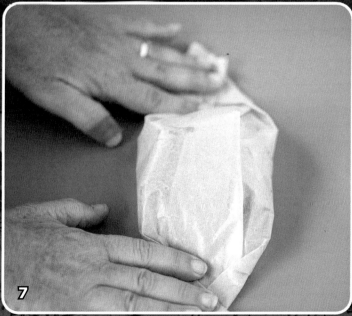

MIDDLE EAST FEAST

TO PREPARE THIS MEAL

YOU WILL NEED

- ☐ Eggplant / aubergine
- ☐ Red peppers
- ☐ Tomato paste
- ☐ Garlic
- ☐ Spices
- ☐ Olive oil
- ☐ Sweet potato
- ☐ Onion
- ☐ Lentils
- ☐ Avocado
- ☐ Kale
- ☐ Black garlic

- ☐ Cauliflower
- ☐ Carrots
- ☐ Coconut milk
- ☐ Cherries
- ☐ Dried apricots
- ☐ Banana
- ☐ 2 Baking sheets
- ☐ Sliced almonds
- ☐ 3 pots
- ☐ Toothpicks or barbecue skewers

- ☐ Steamer basket or metal sieve
- ☐ Vegetable peeler
- ☐ 2 mixing bowls
- ☐ Baking sheet
- ☐ Food processor or immersion blender - Blending is used in all three recipes. Be prepared to wash food processor bowl when indicated or employ a second blending tool while preparing this meal

Imam bayıldı - stuffed eggplant

- 1 large Italian eggplant
- *2 fire roasted or pickled red peppers*
- 4 tablespoons tomato paste
- 2 cloves garlic
- 1 teaspoon zataar seasoning (or 1 teaspoon dried thyme)
- Sea salt to taste
- 1 teaspoon olive oil

Lentil sweet potato green cups

- 1 large organic sweet potato - scrubbed very well
- 1 medium white onion, peeled
- 1 cup dried green or brown lentils,
- 1 tablespoon olive oil
- 1 teaspoon dried oregano
- 1 avocado
- 8 large kale leaves of equal size, washed
- ½ teaspoon black garlic paste
- 1 teaspoons sea salt

On the cutting veg parfait

- 1 cup white cauliflower florets
- 1 cup grated organic carrots
- ½ cup sliced almonds
- 1 teaspoon ground cardamom
- ½ cup coconut or nut milk
- 1 cup dried cherries
- 1 cup chopped dried apricot
- 1 very ripe banana

1. Preheat oven to 400°F.

2. Peel sweet potato and submerge in a bowl of cold water to prevent browning.

3. Fill a large pot with 2 inches of water and set a steamer basket or medium sieve inside it. Water should not touch the bottom of the steamer. Bring to a boil.

4. Cut the onion in half and add it to a pot with 3 cups of water. Bring to a boil.

5. Cut eggplant in half lengthwise.

   Place on a baking sheet cut side down and prick each half skin twice with fork. Bake eggplant for 30 minutes.

   10 min

6. Lower heat. Transfer cauliflower to the steamer and cover the pot. Steam until cauliflower is fork tender (10-15 minutes).

7. Bloom* (see SPICE FOR THE WIN for instructions) zataar or thyme in olive oil in a large pot. Peel and slice garlic and add to spices in pot. Stir to coat. Turn heat off.

   30 min

8. Add the lentils to the pot with the onion. Lower the heat and cook, covered for 20 - 30 minutes or until liquid has been absorbed.

9. Dice the sweet potato into small pieces (½ inch). In a bowl, toss the potato in olive oil and oregano and half the salt to coat. Place in a single layer on a baking sheet and roast on the middle rack of oven for 20 minutes at 400°F.

10. Add the red peppers and enough water to cover.

    Turn heat to high and bring to a boil.

11. Combine the carrots, almonds and cardamom in a bowl. Pour the milk on the mixture.

12. Reduce to a simmer and leave uncovered until almost all the water is evaporated. Add in tomato paste. Remove eggplant when baked and turn cut side up to allow steam to escape.

13. When the lentils have finished cooking, place the kale leaves on top covering the surface of the lentils making

multiple layers if necessary. Cover the pot and turn the heat off. Let stand for about 5 minutes.

14. Transfer steamed cauliflower to the bowl of a food processor and let cool.

15. Halve avocado and remove pit. Scoop out the inside and mix together with the black garlic and the rest of the salt in a bowl or food processor.

16. Stir and cook covered for an additional 5 minutes on low heat.

17. Lay the kale leaves flat on a clean work surface. Remove the onion from the lentil pot. Add the cooked sweet potato to the lentils and mix to combine.

18. When the eggplant is cool enough to handle use a fork to separate flesh from skin leaving the softened eggplant in the skin.

   60 min

19. Combine the cherries and apricots in a separate bowl. When the cauliflower is cooled to room temperature, add the peeled banana to the food processor and blend until you get a smooth custard.

20. Divide the banana/cauliflower custard mixture, the carrot and the cherry mixtures in half and spoon one half of the custard into the bottom of a parfait glass. Add ½ of the carrot mixture and then top with a layer of the cherry mixture. Repeat for the other parfait glass. Refrigerate before serving.

21. Using an immersion blender or a food processor blend red pepper mixture into a sauce.

    Add salt to taste and serve the sauce over the baked eggplant.

   75 min

22. Make two green cups: Spread the avocado mixture on the surface of a kale leaf. Cover with a second kale leaf. Spoon the lentil-sweet potato mixture in the center of the top leaf and roll. Secure with a toothpick. Repeat with the rest of the kale and filling.

MIDDLE EAST FEAST
Home fire-roasted peppers

Referring to cuisine 'of the Middle-East' covers a broad area indeed; There are as many ways to prepare key traditional dishes as there are generations of grandmothers passing their recipes down. Certain ingredients feature so prominently across the spectrum of national interpretations that they - and their nutritional benefits or their stories or both - should make an appearance on this page. The ON-THE-CUTTING-VEG dessert is reminiscent of an Armenian dessert which when translated means 'sweet broth' and includes cherries (sour if we are to be authentic, but sweet new world varieties work great too) and dried apricots. The LENTIL-SWEET POTATO CUPS is Westernized by the sweet potato but kept anchored in its roots with its use of lentils - pulses are often protagonist proteins in this part of the world. Finally, our main dish uses eggplant and it is famed to have made the Imam faint (IMAM BAYALDI means just that). Some stories purport that he fainted because the dish tasted so good; Others push the narrative that the frugal Imam passed out when he learned how much of his olive oil (costly in those days) was used in the making of it!

Fire-roasted red peppers are used to supplement or even replace tomatoes. They are easy to make at home if you have a gas range or outdoor grill

YOU WILL NEED:

- Tongs
- Sealable plastic baggie or sealable glass or plastic food storage container for EACH pepper.

Turn the grill or gas range to high. Place the pepper directly on the grill. Once the skin starts to char, using the tongs, turn the pepper. Continue until the entire surface of the pepper is charred. Keep turning the pepper until it begins to soften and lose its shape. Place the pepper in the bag or container and seal right away. The objective is to have the pepper steam inside the air-tight container.

Remember to turn your grill or range off once you have completed the above procedure with all your peppers.

Leave the pepper(s) in the containers for 2-4 minutes (once you see the bag/container get foggy. Remove the pepper(s) and set aside until it is cool enough to handle. Peel the black, charred skin off each pepper (it should slide off very easily). Rinse the peppers so any remaining black flecks are washed off , slice and remove top and seeds.

Fire-roasted peppers can be stored in the freezer for up to 4 months, jarred refrigerated in pickling liquid (vinegar alone will do) for 2 months or in enough oil to cover at room temperature for one week.

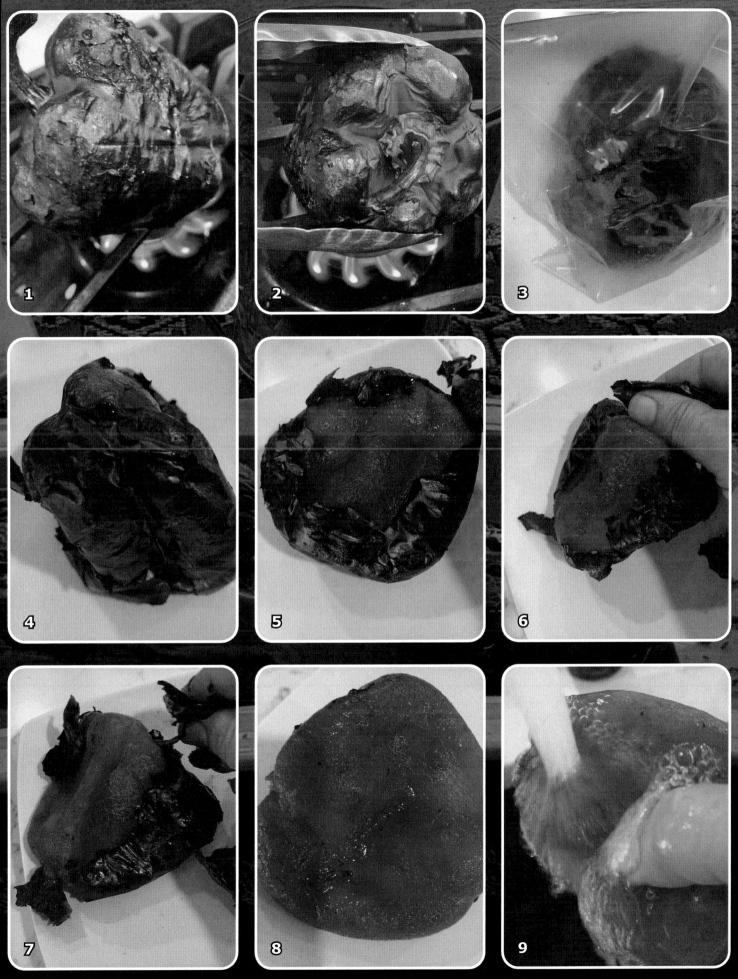

90s NOSTALGIA

TO PREPARE THIS MEAL

YOU WILL NEED

- ☐ Spaghetti squash
- ☐ Onion
- ☐ Ground turkey
- ☐ Olive oil
- ☐ Spices, herbs
- ☐ Crushed or diced tomatoes
- ☐ Vegetable or chicken stock
- ☐ Sweet potato
- ☐ Ghee
- ☐ Unfiltered apple juice

- ☐ Dates
- ☐ Shelled pistachios
- ☐ Walnuts
- ☐ Bananas
- ☐ Coconut cream
- ☐ Baking sheet
- ☐ 2 frying/saute pans (at least one with an oven-proof handle)
- ☐ Plate to fit inside the pan

- ☐ Can of beans, peas or similar (for weight)
- ☐ Mandolin or slicing attachment for food processor
- ☐ Food processor
- ☐ Small saucepan

Squash bolognese baskets

- 1 small sweet onion
- 1 medium spaghetti squash
- ½ teaspoon sea salt
- 1 teaspoon dried oregano
- ½ lb ground organic turkey
- 1 tablespoon olive oil
- 1 cup diced or crushed tomato or _tomato passata (puree)_
- ½ cup vegetable or chicken stock

Sweet potato galette

- 1 large sweet potato
- 1/3 cup ghee
- 2 teaspoon salt
- 1 teaspoon cardamom powder
- ½ cup chopped pistachio for garnish (optional)

Banoffee coupe

- 1 cup unfiltered apple juice
- ½ cup walnut pieces
- 2 pitted dates
- 2 bananas
- ½ cup coconut cream

1. Pour apple juice into a small saucepan and bring to a boil.

2. Preheat oven to 400ºF.

3. Peel and dice onion.

   Cut ends off spaghetti squash and cut into 4 equal size rings.

4. Lower to simmer and stir.

5. Scrape out the seeds and discard. Place the four squash rings on a baking sheet.

   Bake for 40 minutes.

15 min

6. Peel sweet potato and using mandolin or food processor slicing attachment, slice sweet potato into discs the thickness of a coin (not transparent).

7. Stir again. Apple juice will gradually thicken to a caramel-like consistency.

8. Combine cardamom and salt.

   Brush the bottom of a 6 inch cake tin or small oven proof pan with about ½ teaspoon of the ghee. Add one layer of sweet potato discs covering base of pan completely. They can overlap.

   Sprinkle cardamom/salt mixture over the first layer of sweet potatoes. Repeat the process of layering sweet potato discs and sprinkling cardamom/salt. Repeat until all sweet potato discs and seasoning have been used.

30 min

9. Carefully pour the rest of the ghee in the gaps between the layers of sweet potato without disturbing the seasoning on the layers of sweet potato. Swirl the pan to better distribute the ghee. Place a smaller plate or pan on the top layer of sweet potato and then a can on top of that to weigh down and flatten the galette. Cook on high heat for 2 minutes. Remove the plate and can and transfer to the oven and bake for 20 minutes on 400ºF.

10. In a pan, warm olive oil on medium heat and add oregano and diced onion. Cook until onions are translucent but not browned. Remove squash from oven.

40 min

11. Check on the apple caramel and stir again. Remove from heat when the amount of liquid reduced to about 25% of its original quantity.

12. Add turkey to the pan and cook thoroughly stirring until no longer pink. Add the tomato and stock to the turkey pan and stir until combined. Cook covered on low heat, for an additional 5 minutes.

13. In a food processor, pulse walnuts and dates to a sandy texture.

14. Remove squash from oven and using a fork pull the flesh of the squash away from the sides. Squash flesh will be stringy like spaghetti. Create a basket, nest-like base inside the peel round. Spoon the turkey mixture into the baskets and serve.

60 min

15. Slice banana into ¼ inch thick slices. Toss in apple caramel making sure to coat each slice.

    Divide banana/caramel mixture in two serving cups and sprinkle each with half of the walnut/date crumb.

16. Allow to cool, flip upside down on serving plate and cut into slices as you would pie and serve.

17. Top with coconut cream.

90s NOSTALGIA
House-made tomato passata

So many iconic foods of the 90s featured dishes that were stuffed (tacos, potato skins, the dessert that inspired the BANOFFEE COUPE) pie-shaped (quiche, deep-dish pizza or dishes like the SWEET POTATO GALETTE) or involved tomato sauce of some kind! The SQUASH BOLOGNESE BASKETS in this 90s NOSTALGIA meal on a page brings flavor-augmenting, umami-tasting, lycopene-delivering tomato goodness to this decade. Passata means 'strained' in Italian. For the TOMATO PASSATA called for in the recipe you could use a store-bought product, start with purchased crushed or diced tomatoes and blend into puree or make your own passata. House-made passata can be transferred to the compartments of an ice cube tray and frozen for up to 2 months making it easy to add a cube or two to recipes as needed.

Bring a large pot filled with 4 cups water to a boil. With a sharp paring knife, cut an 'X' shape at the base of each tomato breaking the skin but not cutting too deep into the flesh. Use 4 large tomatoes in total to make about 2 cups of passata. When the water is boiling, carefully drop tomatoes in and blanche (flash cook), just until the skin begins to curl back from the 'X' knife cuts. Using a slotted spoon, remove tomatoes from the water and let cool in a bowl.

Once the tomatoes are cool enough to handle, starting at the 'X' peel the skin off using your fingers or a paring knife (it should peel away easily). Cut the peeled tomatoes in quarters and remove the core. Puree, using a blender or food processor. Removing the skin from the softened tomatoes before pureeing eliminates the need for straining.

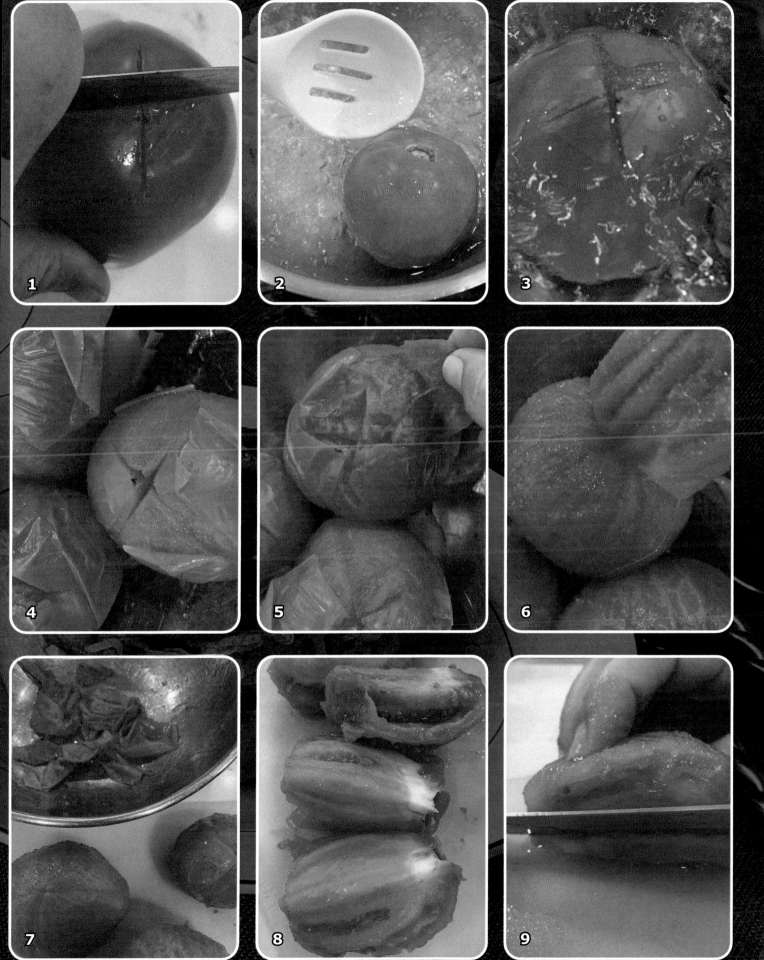

RETURN TO RIVIERA

TO PREPARE THIS MEAL

YOU WILL NEED

- ☐ **Spices**
- ☐ **Chicken thighs**
- ☐ **Ghee**
- ☐ **Red grapes**
- ☐ **Chickpea flour (also known as garbanzo bean flour)**
- ☐ **Oil**
- ☐ **Black garlic**
- ☐ **Apple cider vinegar**
- ☐ **Radicchio**

- ☐ **Oranges, tangerines, blood oranges or grapefruit for citrus puree**
- ☐ **Eggs**
- ☐ **Honey**
- ☐ **Almond flour**
- ☐ **Baking powder**
- ☐ **9 inch Springform cake pan**
- ☐ **2 medium sized skillets or crepe pan with lid***

- ☐ **1 pot**
- ☐ **2 mixing bowls**
- ☐ **1 oven-proof baking dish with lid (or cover with foil)**
- ☐ **Pastry brush**

instead of a pan lid, a large baking sheet can be used to cover while cooking (Food processor is required to make the citrus puree ahead of time)

Chicken filled chickpea crepe with grilled grape sauce

- ½ teaspoon. each of:
- Ground turmeric, ground ginger, cumin seeds, ground coriander, ground black pepper, ground cinnamon
- 1½ teaspoon. sea salt
- 2 skin-on organic chicken thighs, boneless (washed and patted dry) at room temp.
- ½ cup boiling water
- ½ cup chickpea flour
- ½ cup room temp. water
- 1 tablespoon oil (avocado, olive, coconut)
- 2 cups organic red seedless grapes
- *1 tablespoon ghee*

Grilled radicchio with apple cider glaze

- 3 cloves black garlic or 1 tablespoon black garlic paste
- 3 tablespoons apple-cider vinegar
- 1 head radicchio, washed
- 1 tablespoon olive oil
- 1 teaspoon salt

Olive-oil citrus cake

- 11 ½ oz citrus puree*
- 2 eggs
- ¼ cup olive oil
- 3 tablespoon honey
- 3 ½ cups almond flour
- 1 ½ teaspoon baking powder
- Orange slices for garnish (optional)

1. Preheat oven to 350°F.

2. Set a pan on medium heat and add garlic and apple-cider vinegar and stir to combine. Cook for about 5 minutes or until reduced to half its quantity .

   5 min

3. Use 1 teaspoon of the olive oil to grease the bottom and sides of a springform pan.

4. In a mixing bowl, combine citrus puree, eggs, the rest of the oil and honey until well incorporated.

5. Remove saucepan from heat.

6. Fold flour and baking powder into citrus puree mixture and stir until well combined.

   Pour into prepared pan and bake for 50 minutes.

   *Use any seasonal, organic citrus. Boil the fruits - about 1 lb. - whole for about 15 minutes in enough water to cover. Remove from the boiling water and allow to cool before slicing each fruit into quarters and removing seeds. Put fruit into food processor and process until pureed consistency. Using the whole fruit heightens flavor (from the peel), structure (the white pithy membrane) and sweetness from the juice. Tangerines and clementines will make the sweetest cake while blood oranges, Meyer lemons and grapefruits will be brighter in flavor.

7. Toast spices in a dry skillet over medium heat.

   15 min

8. Sprinkle 1 teaspoon salt on chicken skin. Place chicken, skin side down in the skillet. Sear until the skin is brown and some of the fat renders in the pan. Remove skillet from heat and transfer chicken to an oven proof dish with a lid skin side up. Reserve pan.

9. Add boiling water to the dish and cook the chicken covered in a 350°F oven for 30 minutes or until chicken reaches internal temperature of 165°F

10. Slice radicchio in half and remove discolored or torn outside leaves. Cut a ¼ inch slice off the stalk ensuring that there is enough base left to hold the leaves of each half together tightly. Set the radicchio halves on a clean work surface cut side up and brush each cut side with half the oil allowing the oil to seep into the spaces between the leaves.

11. Place a crepe pan or similar on medium-high heat.

12. Combine chickpea flour, room temp water and salt, and stir well until there are no clumps. Add half the oil to the pan and swirl to coat bottom. When the oil is glistening add half the chickpea crepe batter and swirl pan to coat the bottom completely with batter creating a thin but not transparent crepe.

    30 min

13. When the edges of the crepe begin to brown, flip the crepe with a spatula and cook for an additional 2-3 minutes and remove from pan. Repeat with the rest of the oil and chickpea batter. Stack crepes on a plate and set aside covered with towel

14. Sprinkle radicchio with salt and place cut-side down in a hot pan. After about 1 minute turn the radicchio so the cut side is up in the pan (it should have turned from red to brownish) and drizzle half the vinegar glaze on each cut side. Lower heat. Cook covered on low for about 10 minutes.

15. Return the chicken skillet to medium high heat and add the ghee. Place grapes, in the skillet and allow to brown and caramelize.

16. Cover the pan with lid or baking sheet and cook for 5 more minutes

17. Stir to combine smashing the grapes lightly to achieve a chunky texture in the sauce.

    45 min

18. When chicken is cooked, cut in 6-8 pieces. Add to grilled grapes & stir to combine. Lay out crepes on serving dish. Spoon half the chicken mixture over half of each crepe and fold over to create two half moon shaped crepes. Fold the corners over the center and make a roll from each half-moon. Serve.

19. Uncover and serve the radicchio.

20. Let cake cool in pan for 10 minutes and then turn out and serve.

RETURN TO RIVIERA
Essential ghee

Ghee is a kind of clarified butter. The clarification refers to the removal of the milk solids in the butter, which contain lactose (sugar) leaving behind only fat. Despite its cultural and linguistic etymology - it comes from a Sanskrit word meaning 'to sprinkle' - it is used in cuisines beyond the Indian Sub-continent. Its origins in Ancient India are reflected today in ghee being regarded as the most balancing and healthful food in Ayurvedic medicine.

Beyond the clarification, the water is also removed as the ghee is also simmered at low heat for a while. This produces a nutty, almost caramel-like flavor and golden hue. The resulting higher smoke point makes ghee a very stable medium for pan frying. The removal of lactose

Ghee is easy to make and just involves time.

Every cup of butter yields about 12 tablespoons of ghee. Allow 20-40 minutes for every cup of butter

Simmer butter gently on low heat and then skim off solids of pour out clear ghee (as shown in photos)

Ghee can be stored at room temperature for a week. If after a few days on the countertop, the ghee smells sour, skim off the top layer.

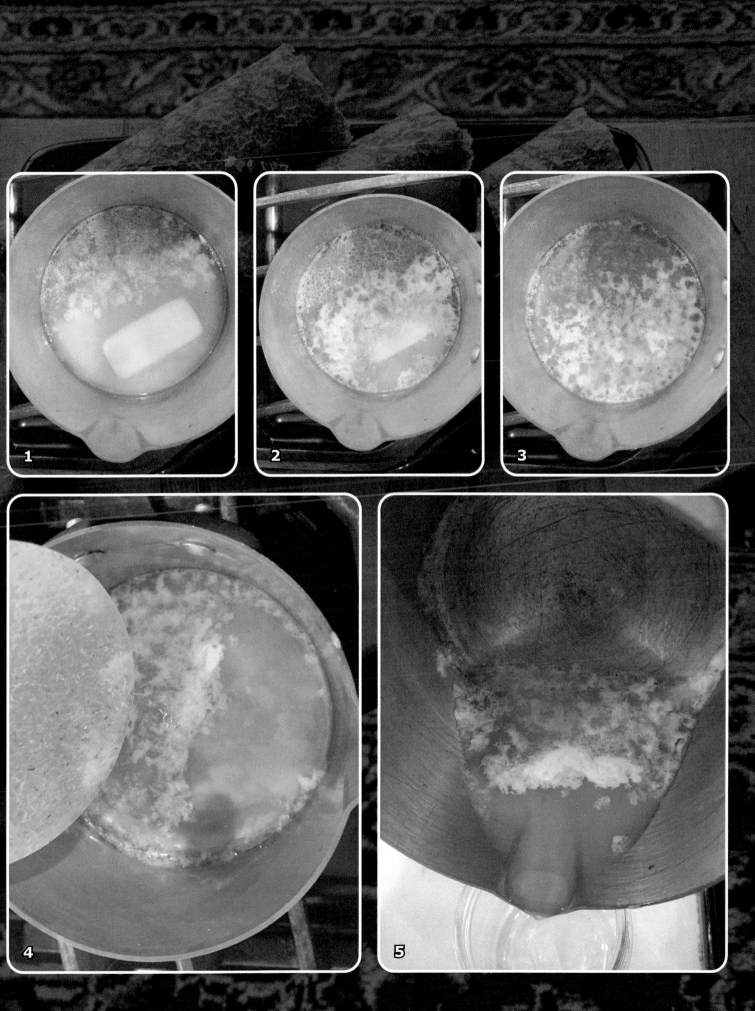

SPICE FOR THE WIN

YOU WILL NEED

- ☐ *Onion*
- ☐ *Coconut milk*
- ☐ *Black sesame seeds*
- ☐ *Spices*
- ☐ *Coconut sugar*
- ☐ *Tea*
- ☐ *Cauliflower*
- ☐ *Coconut oil*
- ☐ *Pears*
- ☐ *Olive oil*
- ☐ *Onion*

- ☐ *Peas*
- ☐ *Squash*
- ☐ *Sesame oil*
- ☐ *Shrimp / prawn*
- ☐ *Stock*
- ☐ *Tea (earl grey)*
- ☐ *1 Large pot with lid*
- ☐ *Food processor*
- ☐ *2 Small or medium skillets or saucepans*
- ☐ *Vegetable peeler*

Shrimp quick curry

- 1 large, sweet white onion
- 1 delicata Squash (or 1 butternut)
- 1 tablespoon coconut oil or ghee
- 1 tablespoon QC spice mix*
- 2 cups chicken or vegetable stock
- 1 cup coconut milk
- 1 cup green peas or shelled edamame
- 6 large shelled, deveined shrimp
- Salt
- * QC Spice Mix:1 teaspoon ground turmeric, ¼ teaspoon each of allspice, cinnamon, cayenne, 1 teaspoon ground cumin OR 1 teaspoon grated turmeric root, 2 allspice seeds, ¼ teaspoon cumin seeds, ¼ inch of a cinnamon stick, 2 white or black peppercorns.

Studded cauliflower rice

- 1 medium white cauliflower or 4 cups florets
- 1 tablespoon olive oil or ghee
- 1 teaspoon toasted sesame oil
- 1 tablespoon white or black sesame seeds

Cardamom-spiced pear

- 2 large (or 4 small) pears
- 1 teaspoon ground cardamom ¼ teaspoon cinnamon
- ¼ teaspoon coconut sugar
- ½ teaspoon coconut oil or ghee
- 1 cup black tea (Earl Grey, Oolong, Pekoe)
- Warmed or at room temperature, not cold
- ½ cup condensed coconut milk
- ½ cup chopped toasted walnuts or oats (optional)

1. Peel & dice onion.

2. Peel washed squash lengthwise leaving a strip of peel every other inch. Cut lengthwise and empty seeds. Chop into crescent slices (if using delicata) about ⅓ inch thick or 1 inch dice for butternut.

3. Heat pot on medium heat and add oil. ***Bloom spices.***

15 min

4. If using full cauliflower head, separate stem from florets and rough chop. For already cut cauliflower, wait for step #6

5. Add onions to pot and stir until onions are translucent (not brown). Lower heat to low.

6. Add florets (and stem pieces if using) to food processor and process until it reaches the consistency of rice.

30 min

7. Add squash and enough stock to just cover contents of pot. Stir. Cover and cook on low/medium for about 30 minutes.

8. Add oil/ghee to saute pan and set heat to medium.

9. Peel and cut pears in half length-wise and remove seeds and core. Set aside.

10. Once oil is glistening, add cauliflower 'rice' and sauté until translucent, stirring(about 2 -3 min). Remove from heat.

11. Combine spice and sugar in a plate and dip cut sides of pear in spice mixture.

12. Uncover curry, add peas, coconut milk and shrimp. Cover pot and let it cook for 15 more minutes.

13. Add sesame oil and stir. Sprinkle with black sesame. Cover cauliflower pot with kitchen towel and lid until ready to serve.

60 min

14. Heat oil/ghee in small saucepan. Place pears cut side down and sear for 1 minute. Turn down heat to simmer and add tea. Cover and cook for 15-20 min.

15. Drizzle with condensed coconut milk and - if using - sprinkle with nuts or oats before serving.

SPICE FOR THE WIN
How to bloom spices

Spices, whether ground or whole (as in for example whole cloves, pepper-corns or cardamom pods) have much heralded health benefits. Ayurvedic medicine holds that spices are generally considered bitter. From a colloquial point of view, bitterness is not preferred in taste or character! But bitterness has a specific role to play regards our digestion and that is to support it by encouraging movement of lymph and fluids and lubricating the digestive process. So, our gut wins. Neither an overuse or under-use of spice from a well-intentioned cook will have a dangerous health effect in the same way that overuse of sodium, fat and sugar will. So, our palate wins.

A way to deepen the flavor of ground

Warm the cooking fat being used (ghee, olive, avocado, red palm or peanut oil are good choices) over medium heat. When the oil is glossy/shiny it is ready for your spices. Add the ground spices and wait until they sizzle, stir then remove from heat until you are ready to proceed with the recipe.

The action of effectively coating the grains of spice in warm oil helps deliver the fat soluble flavors more effectively to the dish and to your taste buds. Depending on the recipe and the quantity of fat used to bloom spices, the oil or ghee you have leftover - if in fact you have any leftover - will work as a great dish garnish, vinaigrette base (see **A VEGAN AFFAIR** for more on

Black peppercorns: pungent and spicy and extremely potent medicinally when combined with ground turmeric

Cardamom pods: sweet and floral; great in desserts to add a South Asian or middle -Eastern note

Star anise: very concentrated licorice flavor. To be used sparingly, whole in infusions or one petal at a time

Cinnamon sticks: warming and carminative (good for digestion) can be used whole in infusion or groups

Turmeric comes from a root but more versatile when ground. Imparts characteristic yellow colour and is known for anti-inflammatory properties. Slightly bitter.

Cayenne: pungent like any pepper but also a little bit tart: adds brightness and heat

Clove: very concentrated, pungent sweet smell, nice in sweet and savory; warming

Ground fenugreek: a little like celery; adds a depth to savory dishes

Coriander seeds: Tastes like combination of fenugreek and cumin

Cumin seeds: impart a slightly floral, very aromatic flavor especially when ground

A VEGAN AFFAIR

TO PREPARE THIS MEAL

YOU WILL NEED

- [ ] **Chick peas / garbanzo beans**
- [ ] **Olive oil**
- [ ] **Onion**
- [ ] **Garlic**
- [ ] **Lemon**
- [ ] **Spices**
- [ ] **Parsley**
- [ ] **Quinoa**
- [ ] **Sesame oil**
- [ ] **Vinaigrette**
- [ ] **Edamame**
- [ ] **Psyllium husk**

- [ ] **Gomasio seasoning (a combination of sesame and salt)**
- [ ] **Orange**
- [ ] **Pepper**
- [ ] **Shallot**
- [ ] **Pomegranate arils (seeds)**
- [ ] **Black Sesame seeds or nigella seeds**
- [ ] **Apples**
- [ ] **Dates**
- [ ] **Pecans**
- [ ] **Maple syrup**

- [ ] **Springform pan (or silicone pie pan or similar non-stick)**
- [ ] **Food processor**
- [ ] **3 mixing bowls**
- [ ] **2 Pastry brush - or wash and reuse one**
- [ ] **Baking dish with at lease 1 inch lip**
- [ ] **Aluminum foil**
- [ ] **Strainer**
- [ ] **Pot or kettle for boiling water**

Split chickpea pie

- ½ cup dried split chickpeas - rinsed then soaked in water overnight
- ¼ cup olive oil
- 1 small onion - peeled and quartered
- 1 medium clove garlic - peeled
- 1 teaspoon lemon zest
- 1 teaspoon ground allspice
- 1 teaspoon ground cumin
- ½ teaspoon pepper
- ¼ teaspoon cayenne pepper
- 1 tablespoon psyllium
- 1 teaspoon sea salt
- ½ cup finely chopped parsley
- 3/4 cup cooked quinoa

Edamame salad

- **Dressing**
- 2 tablespoons toasted sesame oil
- ½ tablespoon gomasio seasoning (toasted sesame seed and salt mix)
- *¼ cup vinaigrette*
- Juice of one blood orange
- ½ tablespoon ground cumin or ¼ teaspoon cumin seeds
- **Salad**
- 2 cups edamame, shelled
- segments of 1 large orange
- 1 red pepper
- 1 large shallot
- ½ cup pomegranate arils
- 1 teaspoon nigella (black onion seed) or black sesame seeds

Glazed baked apple with maple pecans

- 2 large apples (Gala, Fuji, Honey Crisp)
- 5 dates - which have been soaked overnight in enough water to cover
- ¼ cup roughly chopped pecans
- 1 tablespoon maple syrup
- 1 cup water to boil

1. Preheat oven to 450°F and set water to boil in pot or kettle on stove.

2. Drain chickpeas, discard water.

3. Peel, core and cut the apples in half and set in a shallow baking dish cut side down.

4. Brush bottom and sides of a spring form pan with 1 tablespoon of olive oil.

5. Strain the water from dates, retain water and set dates aside.

6. Brush apples with the date water. Keep applying layers until water is used up.

7. Combine the onion, garlic, lemon zest and spices and psyllium in a food processor and pulse until combined

15 min

8. Pour boiling water carefully into baking dish to no more than ½ inch up the apples. Do not wash the glaze off the apples. Scatter the dates into the water. Cover with foil.

9. Bake for 15 minutes at 450F on lower rack of oven.

10. In a large bowl combine salt, parsley, quinoa and chickpeas. Add the onion and garlic mixture.

11. Whisk dressing ingredients together and let stand.

12. Lower oven temperature to 350°F. Knead the mixture with clean hands adding water as necessary, until the dough comes together and is slightly sticky. Press the dough firmly into the prepared pan and set oven to 350°F.

30 min

13. Cut several ¼ inch deep slits into the pie. Drizzle the top with the rest of the olive oil and brush so that the oil fills the slits.

14. Bake for 45 minutes on center rack. Let cool in the tin until step 19.

15. Peel and dice shallot and dice red pepper into pieces the same size as edamame beans.

16. Combine all salad ingredients except black seeds and toss in dressing. Let marinade for 45 min.

17. Remove apples from the oven, keep the foil on.

90 min

18. Sprinkle with black seeds & serve.

19. Lift chick-pea pie out of pan before serving.

20. Remove the foil from the apples carefully to allow any remaining steam to escape. Toss the pecans in maple syrup and scatter on the baked apples.

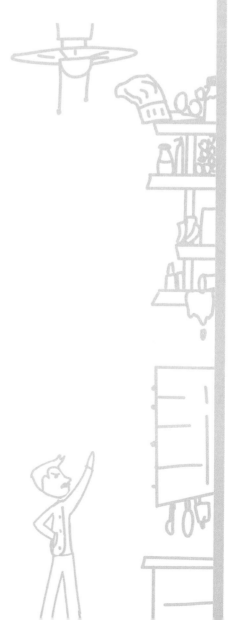

A VEGAN AFFAIR
Vinaigrette alchemy

Vinaigrette is only a little bit easier to purchase than it is to make. So the negligible payoff of time saved is balanced by the cost of a lot of excess sodium, sugar and - to my mind - an aftertaste from added emulsifiers and stabilizers. The trick is to make your own emulsion and skip all those additives designed to make us believe the product is somehow more 'ready to use' than if we were to make it at home. An emulsion is a suspension that allows liquids that normally do not get along to temporarily blend. In the case of a vinaigrette, the basic ingredients you want to have homogenized are oil and vinegar (which plays the part of water in this application, from a chemical perspective). Mustard is a great emulsifier, not to mention a good source of essential minerals and a great digestive aid. It is the coating of the mustard seeds that acts as the temporary (how temporary depends on the mustard used) chemical bridge to blend oil and vinegar. The closer the seeds of the mustard are to their whole state, the longer your emulsion will last. For example a vinaigrette emulsion made with stone-ground mustard will last longer than an emulsion made with Dijon-style mustard. A vinaigrette made with Dijon mustard will stay emulsified longer than one made with American yellow mustard but not as long as the one made with stone-ground mustard.

You can customize a vinaigrette so that it provides an appropriate flavor base for the recipe you are making. For the Edamame salad, in this completely plant-based meal, some East Asian inspired ingredients are added to the vinaigrette base. That would influence the ingredients you would choose from each group (a degree of control not afforded by store-bought vinaigrettes!) You could certainly use the vinaigrette on its own as a salad dressing. A homemade vinaigrette can be refrigerated for up to 10 days. Just make sure it comes to room temperature before you shake it (to re-emulsify it) and use it.

CHOOSE ONE FROM EACH GROUP

4 TABLESPOONS OIL	2 TABLESPOONS VINEGAR
Olive	White
Coconut	Wine
Avocado	Apple-cider
Sesame	Balsamic
Nut oil (such as walnut or pistachio)	Rice wine
Herb-infused	Sherry

1 TEASPOON MUSTARD

Yellow
Dijon
Brown
Red
Stone-ground
Herbed

- ½ teaspoon salt

- 1 teaspoon preferred seasoning (thyme and oregano always good choices if you like them)

½ TEASPOON SWEET (to balance)

Honey
Maple syrup
Coconut or palm sugar
Fruit pulp
Molasses
Jam
Date water

- Combine all ingredients in a sealable jar and shake to emulsify.

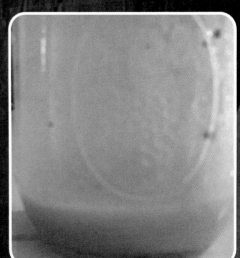

INSPIRED BY ANATOLIA

TO PREPARE THIS MEAL

YOU WILL NEED

- ☐ **Vegetables or chicken stock**
- ☐ **Millet (or quinoa or bulgur if preferred)**
- ☐ **Mint**
- ☐ **Parslay**
- ☐ **Tomatoes**
- ☐ **Red onion**
- ☐ **Olive oil**
- ☐ **Spices**
- ☐ **Chicken breast**
- ☐ **Walnuts**

- ☐ **Garlic**
- ☐ **Red peppers**
- ☐ **Pomegranate seeds AND molasses (or juice)**
- ☐ **Butternut squash**
- ☐ **Pistachios**
- ☐ **Flax seed**
- ☐ **Kale**
- ☐ **Lemon**
- ☐ **Pot**
- ☐ **Pan**

- ☐ **Blender**
- ☐ **Parchment paper**
- ☐ **Food processor**
- ☐ **Bowls**

Twisted tabbouleh

- 2 cups vegetable or chicken stock
- (See WARM WEATHER WINNER for Versatile vegetable stock recipe)
- 1 cup millet grains
- 1 bunch flat leaf parsley
- 1 bunch fresh mint
- 6 Roma tomatoes, diced
- 1 red onion, peeled and diced
- juice of two lemons
- 2 tablespoons olive oil
- 1 teaspoon each of cumin powder dried thyme and sea salt

Chicken in walnut sauce

- 1 tablespoon olive oil
- ¼ teaspoon ground coriander
- ¼ teaspoon ground allspice
- 1 tablespoon ground cumin
- 2 boneless skinless chicken breasts
- ¼ teaspoon sea salt
- 1 cup walnuts
- 3 cloves garlic
- 1 cup roasted red peppers *see MIDDLE EAST FEAST for how to make home fire-roasted red peppers.
- *1 teaspoon pomegranate molasses or ¼ cup pomegranate juice**
- 1 cup water
- ½ cup pomegranate arils for garnish (optional)

Flax pesto on butternut squash noodles

- 1 large butternut squash peeled, sliced lengthwise in half and deseeded
- 1 cup raw, shelled pistachios
- 2 cloves garlic, peeled
- 3 tablespoons ground flaxseed
- 2 cups steamed kale (dino, lacinato or black work best)
- 1 tablespoon olive oil
- Salt to taste
- Juice of 1 lemon

1. To cook the millet bring vegetable stock to a boil in a large pot. Add the millet and bring back up to a boil, stirring occasionally.

2. Bloom* coriander and allspice in 1 tablespoon of olive oil in a pan.

3. Lower the heat to medium and cook, covered for 20 - 25 minutes or until all liquid has been absorbed.

20 min

4. Cut chicken breast into 6-8 equal sized pieces and add to pan with bloomed spices. Turn chicken pieces until seared on all sides.

5. While the millet is cooking pull the leaves off the parsley and the mint and add the stems to the millet cooking water.

6. Remove chicken pan from heat.

7. Place walnuts, garlic, red peppers, cumin and pomegranate molasses or juice plus one cup of water in a food processor or blender in the order they are written above breaking down each before adding the next.

8. Return chicken to medium heat and add walnut sauce. Cook covered for 10-15 minutes.
Remove the lid and simmer to reduce sauce to desired consistency. Let stand until ready to serve.

9. Chop the parsley and mint leaves finely and add to a large bowl.

10. To the same bowl, add finely diced tomatoes and red onion.

11. Wash out food processor.

12. Using a spiralizer make squash noodles or using a vegetable peeler make long squash curls.

13. Once the millet has cooked remove from heat and place a cloth kitchen towel over the mouth of the pot and the pot's lid on top of that.

14. Add the pistachios to the food processor bowl and pulse until broken down into a sandy consistency. Add garlic and pulse until incorporated. Add the flaxseed and pulse until combined. Add the kale and a little of the oil and run the processor continuously until you get a paste. Scrape the sides and bottom of the bowl. Add lemon juice and salt to taste and pulse. Toss noodles in pesto.

15. Combine the lemon juice, olive oil and seasoning to tomato onion mixture.

60 min

16. When the millet has cooled to room temperature, uncover and remove parsley and mint stems and add to the tomato mixture and stir to combine.

*See SPICE FOR THE WIN for how to bloom spices.

INSPIRED BY ANATOLIA
Make your own pomegranate molasses

Anatolia - Asia Minor - comprises the Asian portion of Turkey. Because of its geographic location, many diasporic communities call it home. The ethnicities, faiths and customs of these communities differ but there are interesting overlaps in the cuisine; the pomegranate is at the heart of these overlaps. It is a storied, optically alluring and medicinally potent ingredient. In Armenian culture the pomegranate is a symbol of prosperity and abundance. The Greeks have tradition of smashing a pomegranate on New Year's day and the fruit is often distributed at Turkish weddings. This icon of good fortune also brings the wealth of health to our digestive system and its high magnesium content can help usher a restful night's sleep. Pomegranate molasses can be used to flavor salad dressings, as a brighter tasting alternative to balsamic vinegar. It makes a great, tart glaze for meats and fish.

In the CHICKEN AND WALNUT SAUCE recipe a combination of pomegranate arils (the bright, fruity seeds), and pomegranate molasses may be used or the molasses alone can impart the pomegranate flavour. Pomegranate molasses is readily available in Middle-Eastern groceries and is becoming more prevalent in chain supermarkets in the US, Canada, UK and Australia. The store-bought product contains a significant amount of sugar while the recipe below calls for fresh squeezed citrus as a sweetener (making it more tart than the ready product). To make a sweeter molasses add sugar, honey or date water to taste during the simmering process.

INGREDIENTS

- 2 cups pomegranate arils
- ½ cup fresh orange juice
- 2 star anise flowers

1. Blend 1 cup of the pomegranate arils in a blender and strain out seeds.

2. Combine the juice from the blended pomegranates and orange juice in saucepan and bring to a boil.

3. Lower the heat and simmer until the liquid is reduced to about half its original quantity.

4. Add the star anise and the rest of the pomegranate arils and simmer for another 10 minutes or until the mixture becomes syrupy and dark red in color. If you want a completely smooth syrup, blend and strain all of the pomegranates in step 1.

Home-made pomegranate molasses can be refrigerated for up to a month.

Acknowledgments

Taking even one step - especially the first step - in any endeavor is a complex meshing of millions of reassuring smiles, thousands of supportive gestures and hundreds of encouraging words. I am fortunate enough to have friends so rich in these resources that they are willing to make generous donations of them.

Dana Manoliu - for her chronic compassion and invaluable friendship and for all the times we have cooked together.

Ava Ellensohn - for her beautiful photographs and friendship.

Jarret Ditch - who worked hard in the early days to persuade me I had a ground-breaking idea.

Kate Colter - for her high support surpassed only by her savvy

Kelly and Sayer - who bolstered my confidence as they have always done for my solo projects and for our collaborations.

All my friends who volunteered testimonials, lent an editor's eye and offered diplomatic pause before giving feedback!

My boys, Luca and Gavin - because love.

And my parents - because life.

Interior and cover design by Hamza Azeem
Cover photography by Sharon Mammano
Interior photography by Ava Ellensohn
Illustrations by Luca Cresswell

Tania Melkonian

Eating out, ordering take-away and opening packets were rare occurrences for Tania, growing up. In her family, meals were always cooked and shared at home. Born to emigre parents, she is a first-generation Canadian who understands that food can be a powerful cultural linchpin (a phenomenon of which she was reminded daily as a child peering into her lunchbox and comparing its contents with her classmates' bologna sandwiches!)

What may have caused social discomfort in middle school was a watershed for later in life and guided her ultimate career direction. Her culinary school training and almost twenty years as General Manager of a prominent cruise line's many vessels afforded her opportunity to work with international chefs and culinary brigades. Her extensive travel has supplemented an innate understanding - learned growing up - of the cultural significance of food.

Health of course is another driver of food choices. As a nutritionist, yoga teacher and Ayurveda practitioner, Tania has a strong awareness of food as it informs overall human wellness.

At the heart of it, Tania is a teacher. She has taught cooking classes, lead retreats on fermentation, chocolate-making and Ayurvedic cooking. She has been featured in cooking and health videos and contributed recipes for several on-line health platforms. She is also a food writer whose writing has appeared in national editions of NATURAL AWAKENINGS MAGAZINE, grcenmedinfo.com and boomeranghealth.com.au

Not surprisingly, Tania can be reached at tania@taniateaches.com

Made in the USA
Middletown, DE
17 October 2021